MAGIC WORDS

17 ways to **influence**, **persuade** and **encourage** people to take **action**

by Phil M Jones

INTRODUCTION

The English language is a powerful tool and, when used appropriately, it can ensure that difficult conversations reach a positive, predictable and pre-determined conclusion.

So many of the word choices that I share with you talk to the sub-conscious brain, which allows people to make rational decisions quicker, easier and with more authority. Enjoy using these "Magic Words" and, more importantly, the results that they bring.

Phil

philmjones
helping your business reach new heights

1. DON'T WORRY...

In all difficult conversations it is important that we diffuse the situation as quick as we possibly can. Two words that can very quickly bring calm to a difficult situation are the words "Don't worry". They instantly provide reassurance and turn big challenges into smaller ones. The fact that you use these words and remain composed and controlled in your tone passes comfort to the person you are speaking with.

We are all conditioned from our childhood and have memories of the words "Don't worry" being used to comfort us at difficult times. Introducing these words in adult conversation can trigger the same comforting emotion. These words can be used when faced with a difficult conversation either face to face or on the telephone. They are particularly useful when someone is undecided or has concerns about taking the next step.

Examples would be:

"Don't worry you are speaking to exactly the right person"

"Don't worry we have seen this situation many times before and are perfectly equipped to help"

"Don't worry I understand your current point of view and I am sorry that this is how you currently feel..."

"Don't worry you are bound to feel nervous and that's exactly why we are here to help."

MAGIC
WORDS

2. WHAT'S GOING TO BE EASIER...?

This set of words is so incredibly powerful and relies upon two very simple truths:

1. People like to think that it was their idea and make the final choice.
2. People typically pick the path of least resistance.

They are particularly useful when you are speaking with someone who is uncertain between 2 or more choices and is resisting from making a decision. By prefacing the choices with the words "What's going to be easier..." it suggests that both options will be easy and therefore they should come to a decision effortlessly.

By following this preface with an explanation of each option, you can help the person you are speaking with to choose the right path forward. Explain the benefits of your preferred outcome and just the features and challenges of the least preferred option and the listener will pick your preferred option as it is presented as the easiest choice.

Examples would be:

> "What's going to be easier; continuing to work with us, receive great service and have no hassle or move your services to someone new, run the risk of interrupted services and have an international call centre handle your questions as opposed to someone like me?"
>
> "What's going to be easier; continuing to receive bad service and overpriced products or completing a simple one page form, letting us take care of everything for you"

3. I'M NOT SURE IF IT'S FOR YOU, BUT...

We often find ourselves wanting to recommend something to someone, knowing it may be of huge benefit; yet we struggle to find the opportunity to fit our recommendation into the conversation.

Perhaps we do not want to interrupt, particularly if we run the risk of the other person rejecting our ideas.

Understanding this, these words have been developed to allow you to introduce just about anything, to anyone, completely rejection free. The words "I'm not sure if it's for you, but..." can be used to preface any idea you wish to introduce.

There is absolutely no pressure - you have made it ok for the person you are speaking with to decline your offer and as such it becomes easier to say yes.

The inclusion of the word "but" in this set of words subtly reverses the first statement, so that, with no burden, the customer really hears "I think you might benefit from..."

Examples would be:

"I am not sure if it's for you, but are you free on...?"

"I am not sure if it is for you, but would you be open to saving money on...?"

"I am not sure if it is for you, but have you considered...?"

MAGIC WORDS

4. WOULD IT BE OKAY IF...?

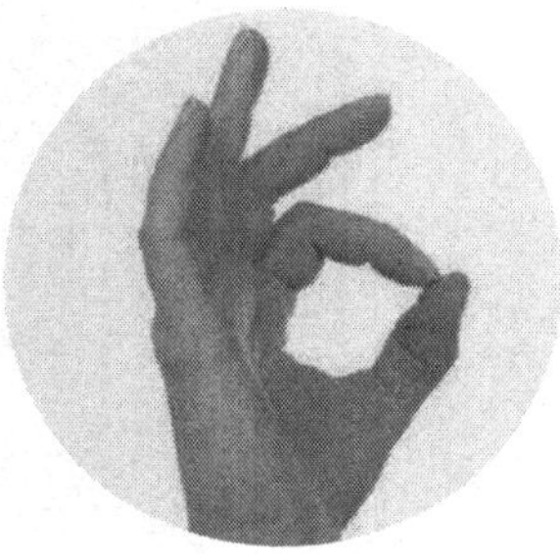

Gaining initial agreement from people prior to defining the action is a very powerful approach when looking to get your own way. Using these words can ensure that your listener is 90% of the way towards agreeing to your action, before they even know what it is.

It is almost impossible to say no to any reasonable request that proceeds the preface "Would it be ok if...?" It can be used to get people to agree to so many things; from appointment creation, to quoting for additional work or perhaps even just buying your self some time.

You can practice in so many circumstances and you will be blown away with the results.

Examples would be:

"Would it be ok if I popped in to visit you next week?"

"Would it be ok if I priced up what we have discussed so that you can make a decision on it when we meet next week?"

"Would it be ok if I take some time to look into this properly and get back to you by the close of play today?"

MAGIC WORDS

5. BEFORE YOU MAKE YOUR MIND UP...

Sometimes our conversations result in people wanting to change their mind or go back on a decision they made previously. In these circumstances, people are typically pretty certain of the outcome that they desire from the conversation.

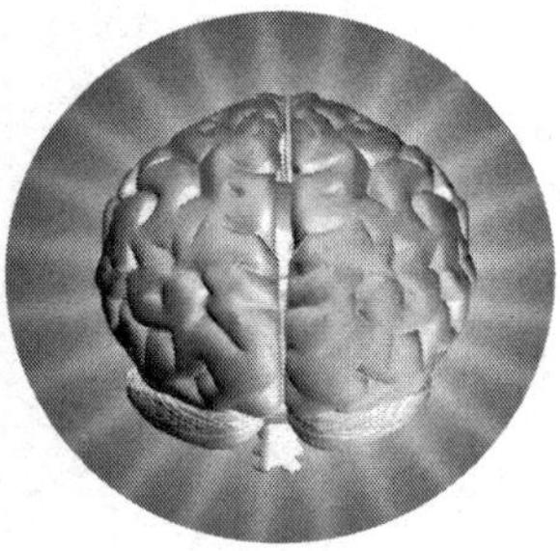

When faced with this situation we can often find ourselves putting up our guard, unknowingly going head to head, firing a barrage of reasons at the person to try to get them to change their mind.

Before we look for them to change their mind we must first change their state of mind into a position in which they are open for change.

By prefacing a qualifying question with the words "before you make your mind up..." you naturally take the decision maker from being certain of their desired outcome to becoming open minded to consider an alternative.

Examples would be:

"Before you make your mind up, have you considered how our services truly compare to what you been offered?"

"Before you make your mind up, wouldn't it make sense to gain all the information to ensure you make an informed decision?"

"Before you make your mind up, shall we just look at some other options?"

6. ENOUGH

If you are looking for decisions based on frequency, quantity or different levels of service, the introduction of the word "enough" can allow you to get more from less in a range of scenarios. Providing you're reasonable, using the word "enough" can stretch the actual outcome ensuring you maximise these opportunities.

Inside everybody's head is a little voice – and if you're sitting there thinking you have no little voice, it's your little voice that's telling you that! Upon hearing "Would x be enough for you?", the brain can only focus on the direct question asked.

As such, they will be able to answer the question easily and positively, which will give you the greater quantity you desired - as long as you don't push too far!

Examples would be:

"Would once a week be enough for you?"

" Is 6 going to be enough for you?"

"We will get that done for you this afternoon, is that soon enough for you?"

7. MOST PEOPLE

Human beings are great at following the crowd and copying what others do. We take great comfort in knowing that others have gone before us and so that makes it ok and safe for us to do the same.

Knowing that people behave like lemmings, when we are looking to get people to make decision quickly we should always talk in terms of "Most people". Each time we talk of "Most people" an alarm goes off in their head, accepting that they are "Most people" and should act as "Most people" do.

This is particularly useful in scenarios of indecision and can typically bring people round to your way of thinking very quickly.

Examples would be:

> "The way we work with most people is..."
>
> "At this stage most people would be choosing one of these two options..."
>
> "Most people in your circumstances tend to go for..."

MAGIC WORDS

8. JUST IMAGINE...

Everybody makes decisions based on emotion before logic. Decisions are made because it feels right before it has to make sense. To help people make decisions easier we must help them visualise the outcome of taking the decision you suggest or the outcome of not taking it.

Two magic words that make it very easy for you to start painting a picture in the mind of your listener are "Just imagine..." Prefacing sentences with these 2 words takes the person you are speaking to back to childhood story time and they very quickly start to visualise the picture that you go on to describe.

These words can be used very effectively to help people see the benefits of taking on board your ideas. They can also be used to paint pictures of more difficult situations, allowing people to picture themselves in scenarios that either are or aren't what they want. They can then decide how to act to achieve their desired outcome.

People will only take action for a potential gain or to avoid a loss. Painting a picture of utopia or a difficult situation will encourage them to make a decision.

Examples would be:

"Just imagine how you feel in X years' time when you are ..."
"Just imagine what would happen if you couldn't ..."
"Just imagine if you didn't do this ..."
"Just imagine what it will feel like knowing that ..."
"Just imagine what you could do with an extra X per month

9. DON'T CHANGE...

When faced with someone who is stuck in indecision, they are often suffering from a resistance to change. For many people decisions are difficult to make and the process can be dragged out if you are asking someone to step away from their habits, typically resulting in them putting off the decision saying things like "We need some time to think about it" or "Maybe next month".

We can help them and guide them to make the right choice by simply telling them not to change. We then just need to help them to realise that making the decision is actually just doing what they have always done.

Examples would be:

"Don't change, continue to ensure that you get the best value for money by moving your services to us."

"Don't change, simply carry on putting your family first and ..."

"Don't change, just keep doing what you are good at and allow us to do what we are good at."

MAGIC WORDS

10. THANK YOU...

Two of the most underused words when negotiating are the words "Thank you" Each time you thank someone you are earning their respect and are humbling them. Providing you don't overuse it and are always genuine with your gratitude, it is a great way to start a negotiation or dispute and is a big step towards a positive outcome.

It should be used as an opening remark in all complaint and cancellation scenarios as well as a great opening when dealing with objections.

As such, they will be able to answer the question easily and positively, which will give you the greater quantity you desired - as long as you don't push too far!

Examples would be:

"Thank you for bringing this to my attention"

"Thank you for giving me a chance to put this right"

"Thank you for working with us up until now"

"Thank you for sharing that with me"

"Thank you for taking the time to help me understand your current situation"

"Thank you for making that payment"

"Thank you for giving us a chance"

11. SORRY...

Another underused word when negotiating is the word "Sorry". By apologising, you show empathy, which is a likable quality that people struggle to disagree and argue with.

Each time you *genuinely* apologise you create the opportunity to present your point of view also. Providing you don't overuse it and are always sincere, it is a great way to resolve a negotiation or dispute and is a big step towards a positive outcome.

Like "Thank you" it can be used as an opening remark in all complaint and cancellation scenarios as well as a great opening when dealing with objections.

Examples would be:

> "I am sorry that is how you feel at this time."
>
> "I am sorry that I was not aware of this sooner"
>
> "I am sorry, I have not explained myself correctly"
>
> "I am sorry that you are thinking of leaving us."

MAGIC WORDS

12. JUST OUT OF CURIOSITY...

In negotiations, our role is to give people enough information to make a decision and then invite them to take the next step. When people are stuck in the land of indecision, we can make some direct statements or ask some direct questions to get them off the fence and help them make their mind up.

This is difficult to do and, for fear of appearing rude, we often feel uncomfortable and choose not to ask, stepping away from the opportunity. By not asking these questions the control always lies with the other person and you are left not knowing what barriers remain.

In order for you to feel comfortable when asking, this simple sequence of words has been developed and practised widely to soften these direct approaches. Make asking a lot easier by prefacing your questions with the words "Just out of curiosity...".

You will instantly feel more at ease when making strong points- without appearing confrontational. You will ask things that you would have otherwise avoided and gain the real answer behind some of those potential objections.

Examples would be:

"Just out of curiosity, what needs to happen for you to commit to this?"

"Just out of curiosity, is this something that you are serious about?"

"Just out of curiosity, what exactly is it that you would like to think about?"

13. WHAT MAKES YOU SAY THAT ?

When we don't get our own way the typical immediate response is to go on a verbal rampage with an onslaught of reasons why they should come around to our way of thinking. The trouble is that fighting fire with fire simply creates and argument - every argument always ends with a loser. As such in the event of you winning the other person loses and it fails to result in a successful negotiation.

When people object, they often object concisely, meaning any response you have will fail to address the actual issue on the other persons mind. By taking the time to clarify the other persons reasoning and point of view you will then gain a clearer alternative opinion and, in turn, will gain their agreement.

The flexibility of these words is fascinating as they can be used as a response to gain more detail and get a better understanding in an inordinate amount of situations.

Examples would be:

"I might be able to do it next year" – "what makes you say that?"

"It's too expensive" – "what makes you say that?"

"It's not quite right for us" – "what makes you say that?"

14. IF... THEN...

We are often looking to help people to make their mind up. This set of words can help ensure that the person you are communicating with will believe and trust the outcome that you are presenting to them, with complete conviction.

The magic words are simply "if" followed by "then". You form a conditional sentence using these words in this sequence, allowing you to place an action after "if" leaving your prospect to believe that the result that follows "then" is highly likely to occur.

Examples from childhood would be:
"If you don't eat your dinner... Then you won't get any pudding"
"If you are not back home by 10pm... Then you will be grounded for a week"

"If you don't take time to revise... Then you won't get good grades at school"

Although the results that follow "then" are not always completely accurate, the success is achieved from the belief that the result will happen. Taking the above examples into account – these are risks most children wouldn't want to take!

Adapting this into your adult life can allow you to make profound statements and influence people in a considerable way.

Examples would be:

"If you take the time to implement these lessons... Then you will be blown away with the results"

"If you decide to install this system... Then I promise you won't be disappointed"

15. YOU COULDN'T DO ME A FAVOUR...?

It continues to amaze me how simple words in the English language can have such a massive impact on the way people behave. One of these word systems is the request for a favour.

Whenever you are in communication with someone and ask them for a 'favour' the auto response is typically "yes" before even considering the request that may follow. This simple psychology can be a fantastic tool in the market place and, when looking for actions from others, it i a great way of getting people committed before the details are provided.
The request of a favour is particularly useful when asking for referrals or creating opportunities to talk to others.

An Example would be:

"You couldn't do me a favour could you...? You wouldn't happen to know just one person who, just like you, would benefit from our services?"

16. I BET YOU ARE A BIT LIKE ME...?

Getting people to agree with you is a very valuable tool in negotiations and so finding words that can get people to do exactly that is priceless.

If you can paint a picture of yourself taking a reasonable action and then ask others to agree with you, this can be a rapid-fire way of getting people to agree quickly.

The words to use to preface your statements are the words "I bet you are a bit like me...?"

People love to fit in with others and often flex their personality in different scenarios. Including a subtle nod whilst making your statement encourages the person you are talking with to agree.

Examples would be:

"I bet you are bit like me and there are tens of things you know that you should do but just don't get round to doing?"

"I bet you are bit like me and always consider worst case scenario before making a decision?"

"I bet you are a bit like me and enjoy the value of having a real person at the end of the phone?"

17. IF I CAN... WILL YOU...?

People have a habit of wanting you to do things outside of your standard processes and procedures. Whether this is to do something faster, wanting more for less or perhaps just some very special treatment. The request for non-standard terms is your chance to gain something back in return.

The use of "If I can... will you...?" ensures that you retain control in the conversation. It shows that you are keen to help, so much so you are willing to bend a little and you can then use the leverage created to seek a fitting reward for your flexibility.

Examples would be:

> "If I can get this done for you now will you be confirming your order today?"
>
> "If we can match that price will you keep your services with us?"
>
> "If I can pick you up does that mean you can come?"

MAGIC WORDS

OUTRO

philmjones
helping your business reach new heights

I hope you have enjoyed understanding these simple word choices and feel empowered to take action, use your new skills and take benefit from their results.

It has been a pleasure compiling them and has taken years of experience to develop them. Please enjoy their "magic" and keep me informed of the impact they have on your lives.

Thanks a million

Phil

ABOUT THE AUTHOR

Since the age of 14, Phil has been practising, developing and fine-tuning his sales process. His vast experience in a variety of sectors has resulted in him being recognised as an authority of sales psychology and negotiation, for increasing corporate turnover and profitability, and business development.

With a track record of progressing processes for organisations at all levels, Phil is acknowledged for his strategic intellect and has been instrumental in turning around underperforming businesses by surfacing new opportunities.

Phil, a regular guest speaker and author of the highly acclaimed Toolbox, has worked with organisations such as

Debenhams and DFS furniture as well as professional football clubs including Birmingham City and Leicester City. In addition he has a wealth of experience throughout the business sector, which includes evolving a large investment property business, before launching his portfolio of training businesses.

To date, Phil and his reliable team have helped thousands of business owners and sales professionals to develop new skills and maximise their potential. Through his speaking, coaching and writing, he has achieved an enviable reputation for developing successful tailored sales processes and achieving peak performance; and has also won a number of awards for his work.

Due to the high levels of success, Phil decided to share this opportunity with other like-minded business professionals by launching the Reaching New Heights network of business mentors, with a team delivering his lessons and coaching business owners across the globe.

Put simply; Phil has accomplished more than most in his fast-moving life. He has developed processes and procedures, which help people to win more customers, who are encouraged to invest more frequently and return more often. Phil is not a theorist, but is a business educator who gives straight talking advice learned from his own experience.

For further information on Phil Jones or to see how he could help you in your business, please contact:

philmjones
helping your business reach new heights

01527 531 393
enquiries@philmjones.com
Visit www.philmjones.com

MAKE NOTES HERE:

MAKE NOTES HERE: